The Scout Law
Quotes for Life

a collection of quotes on the topics of being

Then join in hand, brave Americans all!
By uniting we stand, by dividing we fall.

From the "Liberty Song," sung by United States
patriots during the American Revolution.
It is attributed to John Dickinson, 1732–1808,
an American revolutionary leader.

by
Patrick Flaherty

This book is published under
license from the Boy Scouts of America.
All rights reserved. No part of this book may be
reproduced in any form or by any means without
permission in writing from the publisher.

Editor and photographer: Patrick McLaughlin
Associate editors: Joan Liffring-Zug Bourret
and Maureen Patterson
Cover design: Doug Teggatz

For Boy Scout Council and Troop orders:
Teckni-Corp
P.O. Box 866
Bettendorf, IA 52722
FAX: 563-359-4671
E-mail: quotesforlife@studentsafe.com

Books by Mail:
The Scout Law
Quotes for Life $12.95
Shipping & handling $4.95
Penfield Books
215 Brown Street
Iowa City, IA 52245

Copyright 2002 Patrick Flaherty
ISBN 1932043-16-0
Library of Congress Number: 2002112273

Contents

Introduction

The Boy Scout movement started nearly 100 years ago with the goal of helping young boys face the challenges of growing up. Scouts learn by tackling physical challenges. They learn outdoor and life skills through the merit badge program, troop leadership through advancement rank, and how to become better citizens by working with community leaders.

The basic principles of scouting can be summed up in the Scout Law. Boy Scouts state that they will do their best to be: trustworthy, loyal, helpful, friendly, courteous, kind, obedient, cheerful, thrifty, brave, clean, and reverent.

In a world where many of our most famous movie stars, musicians, and athletes seem to glorify drugs, violence, and immoral behavior, it can be hard for young men to identify good and proper role models. Some of our highest political leaders bounce from scandal to scandal without remorse or consequence. It becomes a difficult and continual challenge for young men to uphold the values of the Scout Law.

It is refreshing, however, that a dedicated group of little-known leaders work daily with millions of our young men. Their influences and training help our young men retain and reinforce the principles of scouting.

What a better world we could make if everyone started the day promising to do their best to uphold the Boy Scout Law in his business and personal life.

Our family has always tried to surround itself with positive messages and examples, and I appreciate the opportunity to share them with you. I hope you will be inspired by the timeless quotes in this book.

—*Patrick Flaherty*

Foreword

Boy Scouts are asked to do their best to adhere to the Scout Law, to be: trustworthy, loyal, helpful, friendly, courteous, kind, obedient, cheerful, thrifty, brave, clean, and reverent.

Motivational experts, psychologists, athletes, coaches, teachers, and parents have known for years the value of positive examples and role models.

The positive expectations expressed in these values raise the expectations of your own behavior. When expectations are raised, it is easier to improve one's ability to live up to these expectations.

This book seeks to provide positive examples through quotations by people from all walks of life throughout history.

In addition to the individual chapters of quotes for each of the Scout Law sections, there's an additional section of quotes for your use. Our hope is that you use them for inspiration, to increase self-expectations, to be prepared, and to continuously improve yourself and your life.

Trustworthy

worthy of confidence;
dependable; reliable

Trustworthy

Honesty is the first chapter
in the book of wisdom.

It is error alone which needs the support
of government. Truth can stand by itself.

—Thomas Jefferson 1743–1826
Thomas Jefferson was the third president of the United States from 1801 to 1809. He was the primary writer of the Declaration of Independence in 1776.

As I grow older, I pay less attention to what
men say. I just watch what they do.

—Andrew Carnegie 1835–1919
Andrew Carnegie was an American businessman and philanthropist.

As scarce as truth is, the supply has always
been in excess of the demand.

—Josh Billings 1818–1885
Josh Billings is the pen name of Henry Shaw, United States political writer and humorist.

Be so true to thyself as thou be not false
to others.

—Francis Bacon 1561–1626
Francis Bacon was an English author and philosopher.

Be true to your work,
your word,
and your friend.

We must have infinite faith in each other.

I think we may safely trust a good deal
more than we do. We may waive just
so much care of ourselves as we honestly
bestow elsewhere.

—Henry David Thoreau 1817–1862
Henry David Thoreau was a United States writer and philosopher.

Believe nothing against another but on good
authority; and never report what may hurt
another, unless it be a greater hurt to some
other to conceal it.

—William Penn 1644–1718
William Penn was the leader of Quaker colonists in Pennsylvania.

Few things can help an individual more
than to place responsibility on him
and to let him know that you trust him.

—Booker T. Washington 1856–1915
Booker T. Washington was an American educator and political activist.

Always do right. This will gratify some people and astonish the rest.

I was gratified to be able to answer promptly. I said, "I don't know."

A lie can travel halfway around the world while the truth is putting on its shoes.

If you tell the truth, you don't have to remember anything.

—Mark Twain 1835–1910
Mark Twain is the pen name of Samuel Langhorne Clemens, United States writer and humorist.

Everyone wishes to have truth on his side, but not everyone wishes to be on the side of truth.

—Richard Whately 1787–1863
Richard Whately was an English theologian and writer.

Good people do not need laws to tell them to act responsibly, while bad people will find a way around the laws.

—Plato approximate life span 427–347 B.C.
Plato was a Greek writer and philosopher and a student of Socrates. Plato's most famous student was Aristotle.

*Rather fail with honor
than succeed by fraud.*

—**Sophocles approximate life span 496–406 B.C.**
Sophocles was a Greek writer and philosopher.

*Hold yourself responsible for a higher
standard than anybody else expects of you.
Never excuse yourself.*

—**Henry Ward Beecher 1813–1887**
Henry Ward Beecher was a prominent United States religious leader
and advocate of ending slavery.

*Oh, what a tangled web we weave,
when first we practice to deceive!*

—**Sir Walter Scott 1771–1832**
Sir Walter Scott was a Scottish writer.

No legacy is so rich as honesty.

*Mine honor is my life; both grow in one;
take honor from me, and my life is done.*

*This above all: To thine own self be true,
and it must follow, as the night the day,
thou canst not then be false to any man.*

—**William Shakespeare 1564–1616**
William Shakespeare was one of England's greatest writers.

*The least initial deviation from the truth
is multiplied later a thousandfold.*

—Aristotle 384–322 B.C.

Aristotle was a Greek writer, teacher, and philosopher, often considered the father of logic.

Well done is better than well said.

—Benjamin Franklin 1706–1790

Benjamin Franklin was a United States writer, inventor, scientist, and Revolutionary War patriot.

*It does not require many words
to speak the truth.*

—Chief Joseph 1840–1904

Chief Joseph was a famous leader of the Nez Perce American Indian tribe.

*Power is not revealed by striking hard
or often, but by striking true.*

—Honoré de Balzac 1799–1850

Honoré de Balzac was a famous French writer.

*Put your trust in God, my boys,
and keep your powder dry!*

—Valentine Blacker 1778–1823

Valentine Blacker was an English soldier.

When you know a thing,
to hold that you know it;
and when you do not know a thing,
to allow that you do not know it—
this is knowledge.

The object of the superior man
is truth.

—**Confucius 551–479 B.C.**
Confucius was a Chinese writer and philosopher.

Beware lest you lose the substance
by grasping at the shadow.

—**Aesop approximate life span 620–560 B.C.**
Aesop was a Greek slave who captured his stories in his book, *Aesop's Fables*.

There are no degrees of honesty—
be 100 percent honest all the time.

—**Brad Harper 1925–1988**
Brad Harper was a family friend from Hutchinson, Kansas.

Self-trust is the first secret to success.

Trust men and they will be true to you; treat them greatly and they will show themselves great.

Wise men put their trust in ideas and not in circumstances.

—Ralph Waldo Emerson 1803–1882
Ralph Waldo Emerson was a United States writer and poet.

The hundred-point man is one who is true to every trust; who keeps his word; who is loyal to the firm that employs him; who does not listen for insults nor look for slights; who carries a civil tongue in his head; who is polite to strangers; who is considerate towards servants; who is moderate in his eating and drinking; who is willing to learn; who is cautious and yet courageous.

—Elbert Hubbard 1856–1915
Elbert Hubbard was a United States writer and editor who died in the sinking of the cruise ship *Lusitania*.

Nearly all men can stand adversity, but if you want to test a man's character, give him power.

Truth is generally the best vindication against slander.

—Abraham Lincoln 1809–1865
Abraham Lincoln was the 16th United States president. His term of office was from 1861 to 1865 during the American Civil War.

Loyal

faithful to the lawful government or to the sovereign to whom one is subject; unswerving in allegiance; faithful and devoted to a private person, especially faithful to a person to whom fidelity is held to be due; faithful or tenacious in adherence to a cause, ideal, practice, or custom

Loyal

I only regret that I have but one life to lose for my country.

—Nathan Hale 1755–1776

Nathan Hale was a United States patriot during the American Revolution. These were his last words before being hanged by the English as a spy.

Mine honour is my life; both grow in one; take honour from me, and my life is done.

—William Shakespeare 1564–1616

William Shakespeare was of England's greatest writers.

A man's country is not a certain area of land, of mountains, rivers, and woods, but it is a principle; and patriotism is loyalty to that principle.

—George William Curtis 1824–1892

George William Curtis was a United States writer.

An ounce of loyalty is worth a pound of cleverness.

—Elbert Hubbard 1856–1915

Elbert Hubbard was a United States writer and editor who died in the sinking of the cruise ship *Lusitania*.

*It is a man's own mind, not his enemy
or foe, that lures him to evil ways.*

—Buddha approximate life span 563–483 B.C.
Buddha was an Indian philosopher and religious leader.

*And another of his disciples said unto him,
'Lord, suffer me first to go and bury my
father.' But Jesus said unto him, 'Follow me,
and let the dead bury their dead.'*

—The Holy Bible – Matthew 8:21-22

*Equal laws protecting equal rights
are the best guarantee of loyalty
and love of country.*

—James Madison 1751–1836
James Madison was a United States patriot and fourth president of the
United States from 1809 to 1817.

*It is better to deserve honors
and not have them
than to have them
and not deserve them.*

—Mark Twain 1835–1910
Mark Twain is the pen name of Samuel Langhorne Clemens, United
States writer and humorist.

Loyalty is still the same, whether it win or lose the game; true as a dial to the sun, although it be not shined upon.

—Samuel Butler 1835–1902

Samuel Butler was an English writer.

Loyalty means nothing unless it has at its heart the absolute principle of self-sacrifice.

—Woodrow T. Wilson 1856–1924

Woodrow T. Wilson was the 28th president of United States from 1913 to 1921 during World War I. He was a driving force in the creation of the League of Nations.

Nothing can be more absurd than the practice that prevails in our country of men and women not following the same pursuits with all their strengths and with one mind; for thus, the state instead of being whole is reduced to half.

—Plato 427–347 B.C.

Plato was a Greek writer and philosopher. He was the student of Socrates and teacher of Aristotle.

One finds many companions for food and drink, but in a serious business a man's companions are very few.

—Theognis approximate life span 570–490 B.C.

Theognis was a Greek writer.

Perseverance is a great element of success. If you only knock long enough and loud enough at the gate, you are sure to wake somebody.

—Henry Wadsworth Longfellow 1807–1882
Henry Wadsworth Longfellow was a United States writer and poet.

The days that are still to come are the wisest witnesses.

—Pindar approximate life span 522–443 B.C.
Pindar was a Greek writer and poet.

Success usually comes to those who are too busy to be looking for it.

—Henry David Thoreau 1817–1862
Henry David Thoreau was a United States writer and philosopher.

Then join in hand, brave Americans all! By uniting we stand, by dividing we fall.

The "Liberty Song," sung by United States patriots during the American Revolution. Attributed to **John Dickinson, 1732–1808,** an American revolutionary leader.

Unless you can find some sort of loyalty,
you cannot find unity and peace
in your active living.

—Josiah Royce 1855–1916
Josiah Royce was a United States writer and philosopher.

We must, indeed, all hang together or, most
assuredly, we shall all hang separately.

—Benjamin Franklin 1706–1790
Benjamin Franklin was a United States writer, inventor, scientist, and Revolutionary War patriot.

What we obtain too cheaply
we esteem too little;
it is dearness only
that gives everything its value.

—Thomas Paine 1737–1809
Thomas Paine was an English-born writer and philosopher who played a significant role in helping the United States in the American Revolution.

To strive, to seek, to find,
and not to yield!

—Lord Alfred Tennyson 1809–1892
Lord Alfred Tennyson was an English writer and poet.

The reward of a thing well done
is to have done it.

It is impossible for a man
to be cheated
by anyone but himself.

—**Ralph Waldo Emerson 1803–1882**
Ralph Waldo Emerson was a United States writer and poet.

Helpful

giving help; of service
or assistance; useful,
constructive, encouraging

Helpful

*Do all the good you can, by all the means
you can, in all the ways you can,
in all the places you can, at all the times
you can, to all the people you can,
as long as ever you can.*

—**John Wesley 1703–1791**
John Wesley was an English religious leader and a founder of Methodism.

*As to diseases, make a habit of two things—
to help, or at least, to do no harm.*

—**Hippocrates approximate life span 460–377 B.C.**
Hippocrates was a Greek physician, often considered the father of modern medicine.

*We always have time enough,
if we will but use it right.*

—**Johann Wolfgang von Goethe 1749–1832**
Johann Wolfgang von Goethe was a German writer and scientist.

*Behold, how good and how pleasant it is
for brethren to dwell together in unity.*

—**The Bible – Psalms 133:1**

*Die when I may, I want it said of me
by those who knew me best that I always
plucked a thistle and planted a flower
where I thought a flower would grow.*

—**Abraham Lincoln 1809–1865**

Abraham Lincoln was the 16th United States president. His term of office was from 1861 to 1865 during the American Civil War.

*Down in their hearts, wise men know
this truth: The only way to help yourself
is to help others.*

—**Elbert Hubbard 1856–1915**

Elbert Hubbard was a United States writer and editor who died in the sinking of the cruise ship *Lusitania.*

*How far that little candle throws his beams!
So shines a good deed in a weary world.*

—**William Shakespeare 1564–1616**

William Shakespeare was one of England's greatest writers.

*If I have seen farther than others,
it is because I was standing
on the shoulders of giants.*

—**Sir Isaac Newton 1642–1727**

Sir Isaac Newton was an English mathematician and scientist. His works led to the understanding of the laws of gravity and calculus.

*If the world seems cold to you,
kindle fires to warm it.*

—**Lucy Larcom 1824–1893**

Lucy Larcom was a United States writer and teacher.

Don't be a cynic…and bewail and moan.
Omit the negative propositions…
Don't waste yourself in rejection,
nor bark against the bad,
but chant the beauty of the good.
Set down nothing
that will not help somebody.

It is one of the beautiful compensations
of life that no man can sincerely try to help
another without helping himself.

To help the young soul, to add energy,
inspire hope, and blow the coals
into a useful flame; to redeem defeat
by new thought and firm action: This,
though not easy, is the work of divine man.

—Ralph Waldo Emerson 1803–1882
Ralph Waldo Emerson was a United States writer and poet.

No man is an island entire of itself;
every man is a piece of the continent,
a part of the main.

—John Donne 1572–1631
John Donne was an English clergyman and poet.

*The man who doesn't read good books
has no advantage over the man who
can't read them.*

*Keep away from people who try to belittle
your ambitions. Small people always do
that, but the really great make you feel
that you, too, can become great.*

—**Mark Twain 1835–1910**
Mark Twain is the pen name of Samuel Langhorne Clemens, United States writer and humorist.

*Success is to be measured not so much
by the position that one has reached in life
as by the obstacles which one has overcome
while trying to succeed.*

—**Booker T. Washington 1856–1915**
Booker T. Washington was an American educator and political activist.

*If we are ever in doubt about what to do, it
is a good rule to ask ourselves what we shall
wish on the morrow that we had done.*

—**Sir John Lubbock 1834–1913**
Sir John Lubbock was an English writer.

*Think that day lost whose descending sun
views from the hand no noble action done.*

—**Joseph Joubert 1754–1824**
Joseph Joubert was a French writer and philosopher.

They might not need me, but they might.
I'll let my head be just in sight;
a smile as small as mine
might be precisely their necessity.

Not knowing when the dawn will come,
I open every door.

—**Emily Dickinson 1830–1886**
Emily Dickinson was a United States writer and poet.

Men are often capable of greater things
than they perform. They are sent
into the world with bills of credit,
and seldom draw to their full extent.

—**Horace Walpole 1717–1797**
Horace Walpole was an English writer.

Men of lofty genius when they are doing
the least work are most active.

—**Leonardo da Vinci 1452–1519**
Leonardo da Vinci was an Italian architect, engineer, painter, sculptor, inventor, and scientist.

Life's tragedy is that we get old too soon
and wise too late.

—**Benjamin Franklin 1706–1790**
Benjamin Franklin was a United States writer, inventor, scientist, and Revolutionary War patriot.

We cannot live only for ourselves.
A thousand fibers connect us
with our fellow men;
and along those fibers,
as sympathetic threads,
our actions run as causes,
and they come back to us as effects.

—Herman Melville 1819–1891
Herman Melville was a United States writer and sailor.

In the arena of human life the honors
and rewards fall to those
who show their good qualities in action.

The greatest virtues are those
which are most useful to other persons.

—Aristotle 384–322 B.C.
Aristotle was a Greek writer, teacher, and philosopher, often considered the father of logic.

The gods help them that help themselves.

—Aesop approximate life span 620–560 B.C.
Aesop was a Greek slave who captured his stories in his book, *Aesop's Fables.*

Friendly

kindly; not hostile; amicable; supporting; helping; favorable; manifesting or disposed to goodwill; kindly interest

Friendly

The only reward of virtue is virtue.
The only way to have a friend
is to be one.

A friend is a person with whom I may
be sincere. Before him, I may think aloud.

He who has a thousand friends
has not a friend to spare,
while he who has one enemy
will meet him everywhere.

The glory of friendship is not
the outstretched hand, nor the kindly smile,
nor the joy of companionship;
it is the spiritual inspiration that comes
to one when you discover that someone else
believes in you and is willing to trust you
with a friendship.

—Ralph Waldo Emerson 1803–1882
Ralph Waldo Emerson was a United States writer and poet.

A clever man commits no minor blunders.

—Johann Wolfgang von Goethe 1749–1832
Johann Wolfgang von Goethe was a German writer and scientist.

Have no friends not equal to yourself.

—Confucius 551–479 B.C.
Confucius was a Chinese writer and philosopher.

Be slow in choosing a friend,
but slower in changing him.

—Benjamin Franklin 1706–1790
Benjamin Franklin was a United States writer, inventor, scientist, and Revolutionary War patriot.

A blessed thing it is for any man or woman
to have a friend, one human soul whom we
can trust utterly, who knows the best and
worst of us, and who loves us in spite of all
our faults.

—Charles Kingsley 1819–1875
Charles Kingsley was an English clergyman and writer.

Am I not destroying my enemies
when I make friends of them?

—Abraham Lincoln 1809–1865
Abraham Lincoln was the 16th United States president. His term of office was from 1861 to 1865 during the American Civil War.

Animals are such agreeable friends;
they ask no questions,
they pass no judgments.

—George Eliot 1819–1880

George Eliot is the pen name of English writer Mary Ann Evans.

Be slow to fall into friendship,
but when thou art in,
continue firm and constant.

—Socrates approximate life span 469–399 B.C.

Socrates was a Greek philosopher and educator, and the Socratic method of teaching was named in his honor.

Friendship is like money,
easier made than kept.

—Samuel Butler 1835–1902

Samuel Butler was an English writer.

An insincere and evil friend
is more to be feared than a wild beast;
a wild beast may wound your body,
but an evil friend will wound your mind.

—Buddha approximate life span 563–483 B.C.

Buddha was an Indian philosopher and religious leader.

Friendship is one mind in two bodies.

—**Mencius approximate life span 371–289 B.C.**
Mencius was a Chinese philosopher.

Be courteous to all, but intimate with few,
and let those few be well tried
before you give them your confidence.
True friendship is a plant of slow growth,
and must undergo and withstand
the shocks of adversity
before it is entitled to the appellation.

—**George Washington 1732–1799**
George Washington was the United States military leader during the American Revolutionary War and was unanimously later elected the first U.S. president. He served from 1789 to 1797.

Friendships are fragile things
and require as much care in handling
as any other fragile and precious thing.

—**Randolph S. Bourne 1886–1918**
Randolph S. Bourne was a United States writer.

I had three chairs in my house: one for
solitude, two for friendship, three for society.

The most I can do for my friend
is simply be his friend.

—**Henry David Thoreau 1817–1862**
Henry David Thoreau was a United States writer and philosopher.

If all men knew what each said of the other,
there would not be four friends in the world.

—Blaise Pascal 1623–1662

Blaise Pascal was a French mathematician, scientist, and philosopher.

The greatest happiness of life
is the conviction that we are loved—
loved for ourselves, or rather, loved
in spite of ourselves.

—Victor Hugo 1802–1885

Victor Hugo was a French writer and poet.

Life is to be fortified by many friendships.
To love and to be loved is the greatest
happiness of existence.

—Sydney Smith 1771–1845

Sydney Smith was an English clergyman and writer.

I hate it in friends when they come
too late to help.

—Euripides approximate life span 484–406 B.C.

Euripides was a Greek writer.

Every man should keep a fair-sized cemetery
in which to bury the faults of his friends.

—Henry Ward Beecher 1813–1887

Henry Ward Beecher was a prominent United States religious leader and advocate of ending slavery.

What is a friend? A single soul
dwelling in two bodies.

—**Aristotle approximate life span 384–322 B.C.**
Aristotle was a Greek writer, teacher, and philosopher, often considered the father of logic.

It is not so much our friends' help
that helps us as the confident knowledge
that they will help us.

—**Epicurus approximate life span 341–270 B.C.**
Epicurus was a Greek philosopher.

They might not need me,
but they might.
I'll let my head be just in sight;
a smile as small as mine might be,
precisely their necessity.

—**Emily Dickinson 1830–1886**
Emily Dickinson was a United States writer and poet.

Courteous

polite and gracious;
considerate toward others;
well-mannered

Courteous

You cannot do a kindness too soon,
for you never know how soon
it will be too late.

Life is not so short but that there is always
time enough for courtesy.

The music that can deepest reach and cure
all ill is cordial speech.

There can be no high civility
without a deep morality.

—Ralph Waldo Emerson 1803–1882
Ralph Waldo Emerson was a United States writer and poet.

*Do not worry; eat three square meals
a day; say your prayers; be courteous
to your creditors; keep your digestion good;
exercise; go slow and easy. Maybe there
are other things your special case requires
to make you happy but, my friend, these
I reckon will give you a good life.*

—Abraham Lincoln 1809–1865
Abraham Lincoln was the 16th United States president. His term of
office was from 1861 to 1865 during the American Civil War.

*For courtesy wins women
all as well as valor may.*

The greater man the greater courtesy.

—Lord Alfred Tennyson 1809–1892
Lord Alfred Tennyson was an English writer and poet.

*If a man be gracious and courteous
to strangers, it shows he is a citizen
of the world, and that his heart
is no island cut off from other lands,
but a continent that joins to them.*

—Francis Bacon 1561–1626
Francis Bacon was an English writer and philosopher.

They're only truly great who are truly good.

—**George Chapman 1559–1634**

George Chapman was an English writer and poet.

Be courteous to all, but intimate with few,
and let those few be well tried
before you give them your confidence.
True friendship is a plant of slow growth,
and must undergo and withstand the shocks
of adversity before it is entitled
to the appellation.

—**George Washington 1732–1799**

George Washington was the United States military leader during the American Revolutionary War and was unanimously later elected president, serving from 1789 to 1797.

We are what we repeatedly do.

—**Aristotle approximate life span 384–322 B.C.**

Aristotle was a Greek writer, teacher, and philosopher, often considered the father of logic.

To awaken each morning with
a smile brightening my face;
to greet the day with reverence
for the opportunities it contains;
to approach my work with a clean mind;
to hold ever before me, even in the doing
of little things, the Ultimate Purpose
toward which I am working; to meet men
and women with laughter on my lips
and love in my heart; to be gentle, kind,
and courteous through all the hours;
to approach the night with weariness
that ever woos sleep and the joy that comes
from work well done—this is how I desire
to waste wisely my days.

—**Thomas Dekker 1572–1632**

Thomas Dekker was an English writer.

Kind

sympathetic, friendly,
tender-hearted, generous;
governed by consideration
and compassion;
gentle, lenient

Kind

Be kind, for everyone you meet
is fighting a harder battle.

—Plato approximate life span 427–347 B.C.
Plato was a Greek writer and philosopher and a student of Socrates.
His most famous student was Aristotle.

A part of kindness consists in loving people
more than they deserve.

—Joseph Joubert 1754–1824
Joseph Joubert was a French writer.

I can live for two months
on a good compliment.

Kindness is a language
which the deaf can hear
and the blind can read.

The difference between the right word
and the almost right word is the difference
between lightning and a lightning bug.

—Mark Twain 1835–1910
Mark Twain is the pen name of Samuel Langhorne Clemens, United
States writer and humorist.

No act of kindness,
no matter how small,
is ever wasted.

—**Aesop approximate life span 620–560 B.C.**
Aesop was a Greek slave who captured his stories in his book, *Aesop's Fables.*

An eye can threaten like a loaded
and leveled gun;
or it can insult like hissing or kicking;
or, in its altered mood,
by beams of kindness,
it can make the heart dance
for joy.

You cannot do a kindness too soon, for you
never know how soon it will be too late.

—**Ralph Waldo Emerson 1803–1882**
Ralph Waldo Emerson was a United States writer and poet.

Genius may have its limitations,
but stupidity is not thus handicapped.

Many a man's reputation would not know
his character if they met on the street.

—**Elbert Hubbard 1856–1915**
Elbert Hubbard was a United States writer and editor who died in the sinking of the cruise ship *Lusitania.*

I expect to pass through this world
but once. Any good therefore that I can do,
or any kindness that I can show
to any fellow creature, let me do it now.
Let me not defer or neglect it,
for I shall not pass this way again.

—William Penn 1644–1718
William Penn was the leader of Quaker colonists in Pennsylvania.

Let us rise up and be thankful,
for if we didn't learn a lot today,
at least we learned a little, and if we didn't
learn a little, at least we didn't get sick,
and if we got sick, at least we didn't die;
so, let us all be thankful.

Neither fire nor wind, birth nor death
can erase our good deeds.

—Buddha approximate life span 563–483 B.C.
Buddha was an Indian philosopher and religious leader.

The greatest happiness of life
is the conviction that we are loved—
loved for ourselves, or rather,
loved in spite of ourselves.

—Victor Hugo 1802–1885
Victor Hugo was a French writer and poet.

A clever man commits no minor blunders.

—**Johann Wolfgang von Goethe 1749–1832**
Johann Wolfgang von Goethe was a German writer and scientist.

Truth is generally the best vindication against slander.

—**Abraham Lincoln 1809–1865**
Abraham Lincoln was the 16th United States president. His term of office was from 1861 to 1865 during the American Civil War.

*The unfortunate need people
who will be kind to them;
the prosperous need people to be kind to.*

—**Aristotle 384–322 B.C.**
Aristotle was a Greek writer, teacher, and philosopher, often considered the father of logic.

*Wherever there is a human being,
there is an opportunity for kindness.*

—**Lucius Annaeus Seneca the Elder
approximate life span 55 B.C.–A.D. 39**
Seneca the Elder was a Roman writer and philosopher.

*Virtue is not left to stand alone.
He who practices it will have neighbors.*

—**Confucius 551–479 B.C.**
Confucius was a Chinese writer and philosopher.

Obedient

submissive to the restraint, control
or command of accepted authority;
subject; subservient

Obedient

I hear and I forget.
I see and I remember.
I do and I understand.

By three methods we may learn wisdom:
first, by reflection, which is noblest;
second, by imitation, which is easiest;
and third, by experience, which is
the bitterest.

—Confucius 551–479 B.C.

Confucius was a Chinese writer and philosopher.

Give all to love; obey thy heart.

—Ralph Waldo Emerson 1803–1882

Ralph Waldo Emerson was a United States writer and poet.

Whoever obeys the gods,
to him they particularly listen.

—Homer approximate life span 780–720 B.C.

Homer was a Greek writer and poet, perhaps best known for his epics
The Iliad and *The Odyssey.*

Doubt is not a pleasant condition,
but certainty is absurd.

—Voltaire 1694–1778

Voltaire was a French writer and philosopher.

If a man does not keep pace
with his companions,
perhaps it is because
he hears a different drummer.
Let him step to the music which he hears,
however measured and far away.

Success usually comes to those
who are too busy to be looking for it.

—**Henry David Thoreau 1817–1862**
Henry David Thoreau was a United States writer and philosopher.

Experience is a dear teacher,
but fools will learn at no other.

Diligence is the mother of good luck.

—**Benjamin Franklin 1706–1790**
Benjamin Franklin was a United States writer, inventor, scientist, and
Revolutionary War patriot.

Reason should direct, and appetite obey.

—**Marcus T. Cicero approximate life span 106–43 B.C.**
Marcus T. Cicero was a Roman writer and politician.

Do something every day
that you don't want to do.
This is the golden rule for acquiring
the habit of doing your duty without pain.

Whenever you find you are on the side of
the majority, it is time to pause and reflect.

—**Mark Twain 1835–1910**

Mark Twain is the pen name of Samuel Langhorne Clemens, United States writer and humorist.

They are able
because they think
they are able.

—**Vergil approximate life span 70–19 B.C.**

Vergil (sometimes spelled 'Virgil') was a Roman writer and poet.

You cannot escape the responsibility
of tomorrow by evading it today.

—**Abraham Lincoln 1809–1865**

Abraham Lincoln was the 16th United States president. His term of office was from 1861 to 1865 during the American Civil War.

We must either find a way or make one.

—**Hannibal approximate life span 247–183 B.C.**

Hannibal was a famous Carthaginian general known for his battles against the Romans.

I'm a firm believer in luck,
and I've found the harder I work,
the luckier I get.

—Thomas Jefferson 1743–1826

Thomas Jefferson was the third president of the United States from 1801 to 1809 and was the primary writer of the Declaration of Independence in 1776.

It takes less time to do a thing right
than it does to explain
why you did it wrong.

Perseverance is a great element of success.
If you only knock long enough
and loud enough at the gate,
you are sure to wake up somebody.

—Henry Wadsworth Longfellow 1807–1882

Henry Wadsworth Longfellow was a United States writer and poet.

Cheerful

marked by cheer or by
spontaneous good spirits;
bright, lively disposition;
likely to brighten, encourage,
and dispel gloom or worry

Cheerful

Few things are harder to put up with than the annoyance of a good example.

The best way to cheer yourself is to try to cheer someone else up.

The human race has one really effective weapon, and that is laughter.

—Mark Twain 1835–1910

Mark Twain is the pen name of Samuel Langhorne Clemens, United States writer and humorist.

Happiness is a habit—cultivate it.

—Elbert Hubbard 1856–1915

Elbert Hubbard was a United States writer and editor who died in the sinking of the cruise ship *Lusitania*.

I am still determined to be cheerful and happy in whatever situation I find myself.

—Martha Washington 1732–1799

Martha Washington, America's first first lady, was the wife of President George Washington, the first president of the United States.

Be content with your lot;
one cannot be first in everything.

We would often be sorry
if our wishes were granted.

—**Aesop approximate life span 620–560 B.C.**
Aesop was a Greek slave who captured his stories in his book, *Aesop's Fables*.

Blessed is he who makes
his companions laugh.

—**The Koran**
The *Koran* is the holy scripture of Islam, claimed to be directly revealed from God to Mohammed.

Happiness is as a butterfly, which when
pursued is always beyond your grasp, but
which if you will sit down quietly, may
alight upon you.

—**Nathaniel Hawthorne 1804–1864**
Nathaniel Hawthorne was a United States writer.

Happy are those who have given up
worrying once and for all.

—**Ovid approximate life span 43–17 B.C.**
Ovid was a Roman writer and poet.

Nothing endures but change.

—**Heraclitus approximate life span 540–480 B.C.**
Heraclitus was a Greek writer and philosopher.

Not knowing when the dawn will come,
I open every door.

—**Emily Dickinson 1830–1886**
Emily Dickinson was a United States writer and poet.

He is a wise man who does not grieve
for the things which he has not,
but rejoices for those which he has.

—**Epictetus approximate life span A.D. 55–135**
Epictetus was a Roman slave, writer, and philosopher.

If I were two-faced,
would I be wearing this one?

You have to do your own growing
no matter how tall your grandfather was.

How chastening in the hour of pride!
How consoling in the depths of affliction!

—**Abraham Lincoln 1809–1865**
Abraham Lincoln was the 16th United States president. His term of office was from 1861 to 1865 during the American Civil War.

It is neither wealth nor splendor, but
tranquility and occupation
which give happiness.

—**Thomas Jefferson 1743–1826**
Thomas Jefferson was the third president of the United States from 1801 to 1809 and was the primary writer of the Declaration of Independence in 1776.

*It is not how much we have, but how much
we enjoy, that makes happiness.*

—Charles Haddon Spurgeon 1834–1892
Charles Haddon Spurgeon was an English writer and clergyman.

*It is not death that a man should fear,
but he should fear never beginning to live.*

*The happiness of your life depends
on the quality of your thoughts.*

—Marcus Aurelius approximate life span A.D. 121–180
Marcus Aurelius was a Roman political leader (emperor of Rome A.D.
161–180) and philosopher.

*It is a rough road that leads
to the heights of greatness.*

**—Lucius Annaeus Seneca the Elder
approximate life span 55 B.C.–A.D. 39**
Seneca the Elder was a Roman writer and philosopher.

*Mirth, and even cheerfulness,
when employed as remedies in low spirits,
are like hot water to a frozen limb.*

—Benjamin Rush 1745–1813
Benjamin Rush was a patriot and political leader during the American
Revolution and a signer of the Declaration of Independence in 1776.

*Repose and cheerfulness are the badge
of the gentleman—repose in energy.*

*So of cheerfulness, or a good temper,
the more it is spent, the more of it remains.*

—Ralph Waldo Emerson 1803–1882
Ralph Waldo Emerson was a United States writer and poet.

*The grand essentials to happiness in this life
are something to do, something to love,
and something to hope for.*

—Joseph Addison 1672–1719
Joseph Addison was an English writer, poet, and political leader.

*Suffering becomes beautiful when anyone
bears great calamities with cheerfulness,
not through insensibility but through
greatness of mind.*

—Aristotle 384–322 B.C.
Aristotle was a Greek writer, teacher, and philosopher, often considered the father of logic.

*The greatest comfort of my old age,
and that which gives me the highest
satisfaction, is the pleasing remembrance
of the many benefits and friendly offices
I have done to others.*

—Cato the Elder approximate life span 234–149 B.C.
Cato the Elder was a Roman political leader and philosopher.

*The most wasted of all days
is that in which we have not laughed.*

—Sebastien Chamfort 1741–1794
Sebastien Chamfort was a French writer and political leader.

*The place to be happy is here.
The time to be happy is now.
The way to be happy is to make others so.*

—Robert G. Ingersoll 1833–1899
Robert G. Ingersoll was a United States attorney and philosopher.

*When one door closes another door opens;
but we so often look so long and so
regretfully upon the closed door, that we
do not see the ones which open for us.*

—Alexander Graham Bell 1847–1922
Alexander Graham Bell was a United States inventor and teacher. Bell is credited with the invention of the telephone in 1875.

*When it comes time to die, be not like
those whose hearts are filled with the fear
of death, so when their time comes they
weep and pray for a little more time to live
their lives over again in a different way.
Sing your death song, and die like a hero
going home.*

—Tecumseh 1768–1813
Tecumseh was the Shawnee chief who tried to unite the Native American tribes against the American settlers' expansion.

Thrifty

practicing thrift; provident;
economical; thriving;
flourishing; prospering

Thrifty

A man is rich in proportion to the number of things which he can afford to let alone.

Our life is frittered away by detail. Simplify, simplify.

That man is richest whose pleasures are the cheapest.

—Henry David Thoreau 1817–1862
Henry David Thoreau was a United States writer and philosopher.

Don't go around saying the world owes you a living. The world owes you nothing. It was here first.

—Mark Twain 1835–1910
Mark Twain is the pen name of Samuel Langhorne Clemens, United States writer and humorist.

How much time he saves who does not look to see what his neighbor says or does or thinks.

—Marcus Aurelius approximate life span A.D. 121–180
Marcus Aurelius was a Roman political leader (emperor of Rome A.D. 161–180) and philosopher.

A penny saved is a penny earned.

Waste neither time nor money,
but make the best use of both.
Without industry and frugality,
nothing will do,
and with them everything.

Dost thou love life?
Then do not squander time,
for that is the stuff life is made of.

Beware of small expenses;
a small leak will sink a great ship.

—Benjamin Franklin 1706–1790

Benjamin Franklin was a United States writer, inventor, scientist, and Revolutionary War patriot.

I not only use all the brains I have,
but all I can borrow.

—Woodrow T. Wilson 1856–1924

Woodrow T. Wilson was the 28th president of United States from 1913 to 1921 during World War I. He was a driving force in the creation of the League of Nations.

What we obtain too cheap,
we esteem too lightly;
it is dearness only
that gives everything its value.

—**Thomas Paine 1737–1809**

Thomas Paine was an English-born writer and philosopher who played a significant role in helping the United States in the American Revolution.

It takes less time to do a thing right,
than it does to explain
why you did it wrong.

—**Henry Wadsworth Longfellow 1807–1882**

Henry Wadsworth Longfellow was a United States writer and poet.

It is not good to be too free.
It is not good
to have everything one wants.

—**Blaise Pascal 1623–1662**

Blaise Pascal was a French mathematician, scientist, and philosopher.

He can compress the most words
into the smallest idea
of any man I know.

—**Abraham Lincoln 1809–1865**

Abraham Lincoln was the 16th United States president. His term of office was from 1861 to 1865 during the American Civil War.

I would rather be ashes than dust;
I would rather that my spark
should burn out in a brilliant blaze
than it should be stifled by dry-rot;
I would rather be a superb meteor,
every atom of me in magnificent glow,
than in a sleepy and permanent planet;
the proper function of man
is to live, not to exist;
I shall not waste my days
in trying to prolong them.
I shall use my time.

—Jack London 1876–1916

Jack London was a United States writer and adventurer.

Brave

not afraid; having courage;
resolute in facing odds;
able to endure pain or hardship;
self-control and mastery of fear

Brave

*Cowards die many times before their deaths;
the valiant never taste of death but once.*

—William Shakespeare 1564–1616
William Shakespeare was one of England's greatest writers.

*A true knight is fuller of bravery in the
midst than in the beginning of danger.*

—Sir Philip Sidney 1554–1586
Sir Philip Sidney was an English writer, political leader, and soldier.

*Ideas must work through the brains
and the arms of good and brave men,
or they are no better than dreams.*

*A hero is no braver than an ordinary man,
but he is braver five minutes longer.*

*What lies before us and what lies behind us
are tiny compared to what lies within us.*

*Peace has its victories,
but it takes a brave man to win them.*

—Ralph Waldo Emerson 1803–1882
Ralph Waldo Emerson was a United States writer and poet.

Courage is resistance to fear,
mastery of fear—
not absence of fear.

Except a creature be part coward, it is not
a compliment to say it is brave; it is merely
a loose application of the word.

It is better to deserve honors
and not have them than to have them
and not deserve them.

Twenty years from now you will be
more disappointed by the things
you didn't do than by the ones you did do.
So throw off the bowlines.
Sail away from the safe harbor.
Catch the trade winds in your sails.
Explore. Dream. Discover.

It is curious that physical courage
should be so common in the world,
and moral courage so rare.

—Mark Twain 1835–1910
Mark Twain is the pen name of Samuel Langhorne Clemens, United
States writer and humorist.

Fortune favors the brave.

—**Terence approximate life span 185–159 B.C.**
Terence was a Roman writer and playwright.

Great deeds are usually wrought
at great risks.

—**Herodotus approximate life span 484–430 B.C.**
Herodotus was a Greek writer and historian.

He who has begun has half done.
Dare to be wise; begin.

—**Horace approximate life span 65–8 B.C.**
Horace was a Roman writer and poet.

It is a good day to die! Strong hearts
to the front, weak hearts to the rear!

—**Crazy Horse 1842–1877**
Crazy Horse was a Lakota chief, best known for his defeat of George
Custer at the Battle of Little Big Horn in 1876.

To fight aloud is very brave,
But gallanter, I know,
Who charge within the bosom,
The Cavalry of Woe.

—**Emily Dickinson 1830–1886**
Emily Dickinson was a United States writer and poet.

I would rather fail in a cause that will ultimately triumph than to triumph in a cause that will ultimately fail.

—Woodrow T. Wilson 1856–1924
Woodrow T. Wilson was the 28th president of United States from 1913 to 1921 during World War I. He was a driving force in the creation of the League of Nations.

The Lord is my light and my salvation; whom shall I fear?

—The Holy Bible – Psalm 27

One brave deed makes no hero.

—John Greenleaf Whittier 1807–1892
John Greenleaf Whittier was a United States Quaker writer and poet.

If we are to achieve results never before accomplished, we must expect to employ methods never before attempted.

—Francis Bacon 1561–1626
Francis Bacon was an English writer and philosopher.

If you do not want to be forgotten, as soon as you are dead and rotten, either write things worth reading, or do things worth the writing.

—Benjamin Franklin 1706–1790
Benjamin Franklin was a United States writer, inventor, scientist, and Revolutionary War patriot.

*I count him braver who overcomes his
desires than him who conquers his enemies,
for the hardest victory is over self.*

*Men acquire a particular quality
by constantly acting a particular way.
We become just by performing just actions,
temperate by performing temperate actions,
brave by performing brave actions.*

*To run away from trouble is a form
of cowardice and, while it is true that the
suicide braves death, he does it not for some
noble object but to escape some ill.*

—Aristotle 384–322 B.C.

Aristotle was a Greek writer, teacher, and philosopher, often considered the father of logic.

*The greater the obstacle,
the more glory in overcoming it.*

—Moliere 1622–1673

Moliere was a French writer, actor, and comic.

It is not the critic who counts. Not the man who points out how the strong man stumbled, or where the doer of deeds could have done them better. The credit belongs to the man who is actually in the arena; whose face is marred by dust and sweat and blood; who strives valiantly; who errs and comes short again and again; who knows the great enthusiasms, the great devotions, and spends himself in a worthy cause. Who, at the best, knows in the end the triumph of high achievement; and who, at worst, if he fails, at least fails while daring greatly, so that his place shall never be with those cold and timid souls who know neither victory nor defeat.

Far better it is to dare mighty things, to win glorious triumphs, even though checkered by failure, than to take rank with those poor spirits who neither enjoy nor suffer much, because they live in the gray twilight that knows not victory nor defeat.

When you play, play hard; when you work don't play at all.

*In any moment of decision, the best thing
you can do is the right thing. The next best
thing you can do is the wrong thing.
The worst thing you can do is nothing.*

—Theodore Roosevelt 1858–1919

Theodore Roosevelt was the 26th and youngest United States president during his term from 1901 to 1909. He is often remembered for his leadership of the Rough Riders during the Spanish-American War. He was awarded the congressional Medal of Honor.

*When a true genius appears in this world
you may know him by this sign: that all
the dunces are in confederacy against him.*

—Jonathan Swift 1667–1745

Jonathan Swift was an English writer perhaps best known for his book *Gulliver's Travels.*

*It is not death that a man should fear,
but he should fear never beginning to live.*

—Marcus Aurelius approximate life span A.D. 121–180

Marcus Aurelius was a Roman political leader (emperor of Rome A.D. 161–180) and philosopher.

Brave men are brave from the very first.

—Pierre Corneille 1606–1684

Pierre Corneille was a French writer and playwright.

Nothing is so strong as gentleness;
nothing so gentle as real strength.

—**Francis of Sales 1567–1622**

Francis of Sales was a French religious leader—the patron saint of writers and the deaf.

My strength is as the strength of ten,
because my heart is pure.

To strive, to seek, to find, and not to yield!

—**Lord Alfred Tennyson 1809–1892**

Lord Alfred Tennyson was an English writer and poet.

It is better to die on your feet
than to live on your knees!

—**Emiliano Zapata 1879–1919**

Emiliano Zapata was a Mexican revolutionary leader.

The brave man inattentive to his duty
is worth little more to his country than the
coward who deserts in the hour of danger.

—**Andrew Jackson 1767–1845**

Andrew Jackson was a military leader who became the seventh president of the United States and served from 1829 to 1837.

That man is not truly brave
who is afraid either to seem or to be,
when it suits him, a coward.

—**Edgar Allan Poe 1809–1849**

Edgar Allan Poe was a United States writer and poet.

*Nearly all men can stand adversity,
but if you want to test a man's character,
give him power.*

*You have to do your own growing
no matter how tall
your grandfather was.*

—Abraham Lincoln 1809–1865
Abraham Lincoln was the 16th United States president. His term of office was from 1861 to 1865 during the American Civil War.

*The bravest man is he who is prepared
to cope with present dangers and to wait
for a better time.*

—Marcus Annaeus Lucanus approximate life span A.D. 39–65
Marcus Annaeus Lucanus was a Roman writer and poet.

*The bravest sight in the world is to see
a great man struggling against adversity.*

**—Lucius Annaeus Seneca the Elder
approximate life span 55 B.C.–A.D. 39**
Seneca the Elder was a Roman writer and philosopher.

*Success is to be measured not so much
by the position that one has reached in life
as by the obstacles which one has overcome
while trying to succeed.*

—Booker T. Washington 1856–1915
Booker T. Washington was an American educator and political activist.

Whatever you can do, or dream you can,
begin it. Boldness has genius, power,
and magic in it. Begin it now.

—**Johann Wolfgang von Goethe 1749–1832**
Johann Wolfgang von Goethe was a German writer and scientist.

The bravest are surely those who have
the clearest vision of what is before them,
glory and danger alike, and yet
notwithstanding go out to meet it.

—**Thucydides approximate life span 471–400 B.C.**
Thucydides was a Greek historian.

The mark of a good action
is that it appears inevitable in retrospect.

—**Robert Louis Stevenson 1850–1894**
Robert Louis Stevenson was a Scottish writer.

To endure is greater than to dare; to tire out
hostile fortune; to be daunted by no difficulty;
to keep heart when all have lost it—
who can say this is not greatness?

—**William Makepeace Thackeray 1811–1863**
William Makepeace Thackeray was an English writer.

We must either find a way or make one.

—**Hannibal approximate life span 247–183 B.C.**
Hannibal was a famous Carthaginian general known for his battles against the Romans.

Clean

gleaming, bright, fine; free from dirt
or impurities; unsoiled; unstained;
morally pure; sinless;
habitually avoiding filth; clever; deft;
having no obstructions, flaws, or
roughnesses; clear; regular

Clean

*What lies before us and what lies behind us
are tiny compared to what lies within us.*

The only reward of virtue is virtue.

*So much of our time is preparation,
so much is routine, and so much retrospect,
that the path of each man's genius contracts
itself to a very few hours.*

—Ralph Waldo Emerson 1803–1882
Ralph Waldo Emerson was a United States writer and poet.

All honor's wounds are self-inflicted.

—Andrew Carnegie 1835–1919
Andrew Carnegie was an American businessman and philanthropist.

*Anyone can carry his burden, however
hard, until nightfall. Anyone can do
his work, however hard, for one day.
Anyone can live sweetly, patiently,
lovingly, purely, until the sun goes down.
And this is all that life really means.*

—Robert Louis Stevenson 1850–1894
Robert Louis Stevenson was a Scottish writer.

Aim above morality. Be not simply good,
be good for something.

Every man is the builder of a temple,
called his body, to the god he worships,
after a style purely his own, nor can he get
off by hammering marble instead. We are all
sculptors and painters and our material
is our own flesh and blood and bones.

If you have built castles in the air,
your work need not be lost;
that is where they should be.
Now put the foundations under them.

—**Henry David Thoreau 1817–1862**
Henry David Thoreau was a United States writer and philosopher.

I would prefer even to fail with honor
than win by cheating.

—**Sophocles approximate life span 496–406 B.C.**
Sophocles was a Greek writer and philosopher.

Moderation in temper is always a virtue;
but moderation in principle is always a vice.

—**Thomas Paine 1737–1809**
Thomas Paine was an English-born writer and philosopher who played a significant role in helping the United States in the American Revolution.

All virtue is summed up in dealing justly.

*Moral excellence comes about as a result
of habit. We become just by doing just acts,
temperate by doing temperate acts,
brave by doing brave acts.*

*The greatest virtues are those
which are most useful to other persons.*

*We are what we repeatedly do. Excellence
then, is not an act, but a habit.*

*A great city is not to be confounded
with a populous one.*

—Aristotle 384–322 B.C.

Aristotle was a Greek writer, teacher, and philosopher, often considered the father of logic.

Cleanliness is indeed next to godliness.

—John Wesley 1703–1791

John Wesley was an English religious leader and a founder of Methodism.

You cannot teach a crab to walk straight.

—Aristophanes approximate life span 450–388 B.C.

Aristophanes was a Greek writer and philosopher.

*Calumny is a false statement maliciously
made to injure another's reputation.*

*Clean your finger before you point
at my spots.*

*God will certainly reward virtue
and punish vice, either here or hereafter.*

—Benjamin Franklin 1706–1790
Benjamin Franklin was a United States writer, inventor, scientist, and
Revolutionary War patriot.

*Be thou as chaste as ice, as pure as snow,
thou shalt not escape calumny.*

*Honesty is the best policy.
If I lose mine honor, I lose myself.*

Virtue is bold and goodness never fearful.

Love all, trust a few; do wrong to none.

Such as we are made of, such we be.

—William Shakespeare 1564–1616
William Shakespeare was one of England's greatest writers.

I am speaking now of the highest duty
we owe our friends, the noblest, the most
sacred—that of keeping their own
nobleness, goodness, pure and incorrupt.
If we let our friend become cold and selfish
and exacting without a remonstrance,
we are no true lover, no true friend.

—Harriet Beecher Stowe 1811–1896

Harriet Beecher Stowe was a United States writer and anti-slavery advocate. Her book *Uncle Tom's Cabin* played a large part in hardening Northern attitudes against slavery prior to the American Civil War.

Sincerity and truth are the basis
of every virtue.

Think no vice so small that you may
commit it, and no virtue so small
that you may overlook it.

The superior man thinks always of virtue;
the common man thinks of comfort.

Virtue is not left to stand alone.
He who practices it will have neighbors.

—Confucius 551–479 B.C.

Confucius was a Chinese writer and philosopher.

It has been my experience that folks
who have no vices have very few virtues.

Whatever you are, be a good one.

—Abraham Lincoln 1809–1865
Abraham Lincoln was the 16th United States president. His term of office was from 1861 to 1865 during the American Civil War.

My strength has the strength of ten
because my heart is pure.

—Lord Alfred Tennyson 1809–1892
Lord Alfred Tennyson was an English writer and poet.

I hope I shall possess firmness and virtue
enough to maintain what I consider
the most enviable of all titles,
the character of an honest man.

—George Washington 1732–1799
George Washington was the United States military leader during the American Revolutionary War and was unanimously later elected president, serving from 1789 to 1797.

Virtue is its own reward.

Honor is the reward of virtue.

Ability without honor is useless.

—Marcus T. Cicero approximate life span 106–43 B.C.
Marcus T. Cicero was a Roman writer and politician.

*It is better to deserve an honor
and not receive it
than to receive one
and not deserve it!*

*It is by the goodness of God
that in our country we have those three
unspeakably precious things: freedom
of speech, freedom of conscience, and the
prudence never to practice either of them.*

*You cannot depend on your eyes
when your imagination is out of focus.*

—**Mark Twain 1835–1910**

Mark Twain is the pen name of Samuel Langhorne Clemens, United States writer and humorist.

*Many a man's reputation would not know
his character if they met on the street.*

—**Elbert Hubbard 1856–1915**

Elbert Hubbard was a United States writer and editor who died in the sinking of the cruise ship *Lusitania*.

*Let everyone sweep in front of his own door,
and the whole world will be clean.*

—**Johann Wolfgang von Goethe 1749–1832**

Johann Wolfgang von Goethe was a German writer and scientist.

*Neither fire nor wind, birth nor death
can erase our good deeds.*

*On life's journey faith is nourishment,
virtuous deeds are a shelter,
wisdom is the light by day, and right
mindfulness is the protection by night.
If a man lives a pure life,
nothing can destroy him.*

—**Buddha approximate life span 563–483 B.C.**
Buddha was an Indian philosopher and religious leader.

*See that each hour's feelings and thoughts
and actions are pure and true; then your life
will be, also.*

—**Henry Ward Beecher 1813–1887**
Henry Ward Beecher was a prominent United States religious leader
and advocate of ending slavery.

He who stops being better stops being good.

—**Oliver Cromwell 1599–1658**
Oliver Cromwell was an English general and politician, serving as the
first Lord Protector of England from 1653 to 1658.

Very wise is he that can know himself.

—**Geoffrey Chaucer approximate life span 1342–1400**
Geoffrey Chaucer was an English writer and poet. One of his most
famous works was the book *Canterbury Tales*.

Knowledge may give weight,
but accomplishments give luster,
and many more people see than weigh.

—The Earl of Chesterfield 1694–1773
The Earl of Chesterfield was an English politician.

Power is not revealed by striking hard
or often, but by striking true.

—Honoré de Balzac 1799–1850
Honoré de Balzac was a French writer.

The universe is change;
our life is what our thoughts make it.

—Marcus Aurelius approximate life span A.D. 121–180
Marcus Aurelius was a Roman political leader (emperor of Rome A.D. 161–180) and philosopher.

Great minds have purposes,
others have wishes.

—Washington Irving 1783–1859
Washington Irving was a United States writer and historian.

Consistency is the foundation of virtue.

—Francis Bacon 1561–1626
Francis Bacon was an English writer and philosopher.

*The most spiritual human beings,
assuming they are the most courageous,
also experience by far the most painful
tragedies, but it is precisely for this reason
that they honor life, because it brings
against them its most formidable weapons.*

—**Friedrich Nietzsche 1844–1900**
Friedrich Nietzsche was a German philosopher.

*Withdraw into yourself and look. And if
you do not find yourself beautiful yet,
act as does the creator of a statue that is
to be made beautiful: He cuts away here,
he smoothes there, he makes this line lighter,
this other purer, until a lovely face
has grown his work. So do you also:
Cut away all that is excessive,
straighten all that is crooked,
bring light to all that is overcast,
labor to make all one glow or beauty
and never cease chiseling your statue,
until there shall shine out on you from it
the godlike splendor of virtue,
until you see the perfect goodness
surely established in the stainless shrine.*

—**Plotinus approximate life span A.D. 205–270**
Plotinus was a Roman writer and philosopher.

Reverent

feeling, showing, or characterized by reverence; feeling or attitude of deep respect, love, and awe, as for something sacred; veneration; a manifestation of this, specifically: a bow, curtsy, or similar gesture of respect; obeisance; the state of being revered

Reverent

Preach the Gospel all the time;
if necessary, use words.

—St. Francis of Assisi approximate life span 1181–1226
St. Francis of Assisi was an Italian monk and the patron saint of merchants.

Nature does nothing uselessly.

—Aristotle 384–322 B.C.
Aristotle was a Greek writer, teacher, and philosopher, often considered the father of logic.

Faith is to believe what we do not see,
and the reward of this faith is to see
what we believe.

—St. Augustine 354–430
St. Augustine was a writer and religious leader.

Believe nothing against another
but on good authority.
Nor report what may hurt another,
unless it be a greater hurt to some other
to conceal it.

—William Penn 1644–1718
William Penn was the leader of Quaker colonists in Pennsylvania.

*Every man is his own doctor of divinity,
in the last resort.*

—Robert Louis Stevenson 1850–1894
Robert Louis Stevenson was a Scottish writer.

*Man shall not live by bread alone,
but by every word that proceedeth
out of the mouth of God.*

—The Holy Bible – Matt. 4:4

*If you can not find the truth
right where you are,
where else do you expect to find it?*

—Ralph Waldo Emerson 1803–1882
Ralph Waldo Emerson was a United States writer and poet.

*God is the brave man's hope
and not the coward's excuse.*

—Plutarch approximate life span A.D. 46–120
Plutarch was a Greek writer and philosopher.

*We can easily forgive a child
who is afraid of the dark;
the real tragedy is when men
are afraid of the light.*

—Plato approximate life span 427–347 B.C.
Plato was a Greek writer and philosopher. A student of Socrates, his most famous student was Aristotle.

If God did not exist,
it would be necessary to invent Him.

—**Voltaire 1694–1778**

Voltaire was a French writer and philosopher.

To live is so startling
it leaves little time
for anything else.

—**Emily Dickinson 1830–1886**

Emily Dickinson was a United States writer and poet.

We had the sky up there, all speckled
with stars, and we used to lay on our backs
and look up at them, and discuss
whether they was made or just happened.

—**Mark Twain 1835–1910**

Mark Twain was the pen name of Samuel Langhorne Clemens, United States writer and humorist.

The Lord is my light and my salvation;
whom shall I fear?

—**The Bible – Psalm 27**

We have just enough religion
to make us hate, but not enough
to make us love one another.

—**Jonathan Swift 1667–1745**

Jonathan Swift was an English writer perhaps best known for his book *Gulliver's Travels*.

Prayer indeed is good,
but while calling on the gods
a man should himself lend a hand.

—**Hippocrates approximate life span 460–377 B.C.**
Hippocrates was a Greek physician, often considered the father of
modern medicine.

The strength of a man consists
in finding out the way God is going,
and going that way.

—**Henry Ward Beecher 1813–1887**
Henry Ward Beecher was a prominent United States religious leader
and advocate of ending slavery.

There are no eternal facts,
as there are no absolute truths.

—**Friedrich Nietzsche 1844–1900**
Friedrich Nietzsche was a German philosopher.

There are more things
in heaven and earth,
Horatio,
than are dreamt of
in your philosophy.

—**William Shakespeare 1564–1616**
William Shakespeare was one of England's greatest writers.

A long habit
of not thinking a thing wrong
gives it a superficial appearance
of being right.

My country is the world
and my religion is to do good.

—Thomas Paine 1737–1809

Thomas Paine was an English-born writer and philosopher who played a significant role in helping the United States in the American Revolution.

Whatever is begun in anger ends in shame.

—Benjamin Franklin 1706–1790

Benjamin Franklin was a United States writer, inventor, scientist, and patriot during the Revolutionary War.

Heaven is under our feet
as well as over our heads.

—Henry David Thoreau 1817–1862

Henry David Thoreau was a United States writer and philosopher.

The unexamined life is not worth living.

—Socrates approximate life span 469–399 B.C.

Socrates was a Greek philosopher and educator. The Socratic method of teaching was named in his honor.

Have not I commanded thee?
Be strong and of a good courage;
be not afraid, neither be thou dismayed;
for the Lord thy God is with thee
whithersoever thou goest.

—The Bible – Joshua 1:9